First foods

To my children, Nicholas, Lara and Scarlett

ANNABEL KARMEL'S FAVOURITES

First foods

*Recipes and advice
to help you wean
your baby*

annabel karmel

1 3 5 7 9 10 8 6 4 2

Text copyright © Annabel Karmel 1991, 2001, 2005, 2011, 2013
Photographs copyright © Dave King 2001, 2005, 2011, 2013
except pages 28, 45 Daniel Pangbourne 2001
This edition copyright © Eddison Sadd Editions 2013

The Random House Group Limited Reg. No. 954009

A CIP catalogue record for this book is available from the British Library

ISBN: 978-009-195576-2

Printed in Hong Kong

Eddison•Sadd Editions
CREATIVE DIRECTOR Nick Eddison   INDEXER Dorothy Frame
SENIOR EDITOR Katie Golsby   DESIGNER Brazzle Atkins
PROOFREADER Nikky Twyman   ILLUSTRATIONS Nadine Wikenden
PRODUCTION Sarah Rooney
COVER PHOTOGRAPHY Dave King

Notes on the text:
- For fan-assisted ovens, reduce the temperature by 20°C.
- All black pepper is freshly ground.

Contents

Introduction

The UK Department of Health recommendations state that babies should be weaned from around six months old. However, some parents feel that their babies are ready before then. If this is the case with your baby, it's acceptable to introduce solids earlier, but not before the age of seventeen weeks, as his gastrointestinal function won't have fully matured. Every baby is different and some will be ready earlier than others. In families with a history of food allergy, hay fever, eczema or asthma, it's best to try to exclusively breastfeed for the first six months.

The importance of milk
When you start weaning your baby, milk will still form a major part of her diet. Whether she's breastfed or bottle fed, milk will provide all the nutrients she needs. Babies should continue to have breast or formula milk throughout the first year. From four to six months, they should have 500–600 ml (17–21 fl oz) of breast or formula milk each day. Up to the age of eight months, milk feeds should be given four times a day. Cow's milk

and goat's milk aren't suitable alternatives to breast or formula milk before one year, as they don't contain sufficient iron and other nutrients. However, they can be used in cooking or with cereal from six months. Use full-fat milk, as babies need the calories for growth.

Occasionally, parents make the mistake of giving their babies solid food when they're hungry, when what they actually need is an additional milk feed. If milk feeds are dramatically reduced once you start giving solids, your baby won't get the nutrients that she needs. Plus, giving a baby too much solid food too quickly may lead to constipation. First foods are more about introducing food than giving a full meal; milk still has an important role to play. As well as experiencing new tastes and textures, your baby will learn to use her mouth muscles, get used to bulkier food and take on more nutrients.

The best first foods for your baby

First foods should be simple, easy to digest and unlikely to provoke an allergic reaction. Start with a single ingredient, ideally a fruit or vegetable. Root vegetables like carrots, sweet potato and butternut squash are very popular first foods; they have a naturally sweet flavour and can easily be puréed to a smooth texture. Mix them with a little breast or formula milk to ease the transition.

It's important to choose fruits that are ripe, with a good flavour; taste them yourself before giving them to your baby.

First vegetables
Carrot • potato • swede • parsnip • pumpkin • butternut squash • sweet potato

First fruit
Apple • pear • banana • papaya • avocado

Banana, papaya and avocado don't require cooking, provided they are ripe. They can be puréed or mashed on their own, or together with a little breast or formula milk. Bananas aren't suitable for freezing.

Bananas and avocado make the perfect convenience food, as they come with their own packaging! These nutritious fruits are easy to mash with a fork; if you warm a peeled banana in a microwave, it's even easier, but make sure it's cool before giving it to your baby.

Baby rice
Baby rice is another good first food; its milky taste makes an easy transition to solids. Check the packaging to ensure you choose one

that's sugar free and enriched with vitamins and iron. Mix it with water, or breast or formula milk, or combine it with a fruit or vegetable purée.

After first tastes
Around five or six months, once first tastes have been accepted (and depending on your baby's age when you started weaning), you can start to combine flavours and be a bit more adventurous with the foods you offer. Green vegetables are full of important nutrients and can be mixed with root vegetables such as sweet potato or carrot, to give them a sweeter taste.

After first vegetables
Courgette • cauliflower • broccoli • peas • spinach • sweetcorn

After first fruit
Berries (such as blueberries, strawberries and raspberries) • mango • plum • peach

The advantages of home-made baby food
Making food for your baby can be quite daunting, but it's a great way to ensure that he's getting good-quality food, made with fresh,

nutritious ingredients. Making purées can also work out cheaper than buying ready-made baby food.

It's important to introduce a wide range of foods from a young age, not only to provide a healthy variety of nutrients, but also to familiarize him with different flavours, and therefore make the transition to adult food easier.

Home-made purées often have more flavour and contain more vitamins than commercial jars of baby food, because they are freshly prepared. Of course, when you're busy, or feeding your baby while you're away from home, ready-made purées are very convenient. There is nothing wrong with feeding them to your baby, as long as they form part of a diet made up largely of fresh food. I believe children are less likely to become fussy eaters if they're used to the varied flavours of fresh foods at an early age. Plus, some babies who are given a lot of baby food from jars become increasingly reluctant to try 'real' food when it's offered.

It's easy to prepare vegetables for your baby's purées alongside those you are preparing for the family meal. Many of the purée combinations in this book are so tasty that, with the addition of extra stock and seasoning, they can be turned into delicious soups, stews or sauces for the rest of the family.

Judging quantities

It's difficult to predict how much a baby will eat, since their appetites and needs will all be different. As a rough guide, you will probably find that, to begin with, your baby will only take one or two teaspoons of purée, so allow about one tablespoon or one ice-cube portion (*see page 18*). As your baby develops, increase the quantity by one or two teaspoons at a time, until her interest starts to wane. Babies have a strong sense of appetite, eating when they're hungry and stopping when they're not; use this as a way to gauge what to give your baby. Providing she's gaining weight and has plenty of energy, you can rest assured that she's doing fine. If she has an insatiable appetite and you're worried about her weight, seek professional advice.

Texture

To begin with, purées should be quite runny, with the consistency of a thick soup or yoghurt, and made up of only one or two ingredients. Your baby's purées shouldn't contain any tap water that hasn't been boiled; you can use the water from the bottom of the steamer, cooking liquid from boiling vegetables, or your baby's usual milk. You can thin purées by adding extra cooking liquid or milk, and thicken them by stirring in a little baby rice.

Food temperature

A baby's mouth is more sensitive to heat than an adult's, and food should be given lukewarm or at room temperature. If you reheat food in a microwave, heat until piping hot all the way through, allow to cool, then stir thoroughly to get rid of any hot spots. Always check the temperature before giving the food to your baby.

Foods to avoid in the first year

Certain foods are unsuitable to give to babies. The following foods should be avoided until your baby is at least twelve months old:

Salt • sugar • pâté • shellfish • spices • smoked foods • soft/ blue cheese • honey

Honey

In rare cases, honey can contain a type of bacteria which, if ingested by a baby under the age of one year, may produce toxins in the intestine that can result in a potentially serious illness called 'infant botulism'.

When to give feeds

Try to make feeding a special time to share with your baby, rather than a chore, so pick a time of day when you're not rushed or likely to be distracted. It's good to establish some kind of routine early on, so try to feed around the same times each day. Young babies are used to food coming in a non-stop steady stream, and sometimes find the gaps between spoonfuls annoying. When you first start weaning, it may be a good idea to give your baby a little milk before his solids, so he's not frantically hungry, or he may become frustrated.

To begin with, give one feed a day – around midday is often a good time – then gradually increase to three feeds (breakfast, lunch and dinner).

Always introduce new foods at breakfast or lunchtime; never supper. This way, if she has an allergic reaction or tummy upset, it is less likely to occur in the middle of the night.

How to feed your baby

Make feeding a bonding experience by sitting your baby on your lap or in a baby chair, where you can connect with her by smiling and talking to her. Always test the food temperature before giving it to your baby.

For the first few weeks, it's not a good idea to give mixtures of foods, other than baby rice mixed with a fruit or vegetable purée. Weaning is a good time to discover if there are any foods that your baby doesn't tolerate well; if foods are mixed together, it's hard to tell which foods are causing a problem.

Food rejection

Avoid making a fuss if your baby won't eat, and try to stay relaxed. If solids are initially refused, you could wait for a couple of days, then try again, or prepare a runnier purée that is easier for your baby to swallow. You could also try dipping a clean finger in the purée and letting your baby suck it off your finger, as some babies don't like the feeling of a spoon in their mouth to begin with. If your baby only takes a tiny amount, try not to draw out mealtimes in an attempt to get him to eat more. Babies tend to know when they've had enough.

Recipe information

Each recipe is accompanied by helpful information on preparation and cooking times, how many portions the recipe makes and whether it's suitable for freezing. Preparation times and portion quantities should be used as a guide only, as these will vary.

On pages 60–61 and 92–3, you will find meal planners to help you through the early stages of weaning. These are intended to be used for guidance; you can, of course, use different recipes if you wish.

Equipment

Steamer Steaming is one of the best ways to preserve nutrients. It's also a quick and easy cooking method for vegetables that don't take long to cook, especially delicate vegetables like broccoli or mangetout. A multi-layered steamer allows you to cook several foods at once.

Electric hand blender Ideal for puréeing food, and easy to wash up.

Food processor Good for when you're making large batches of purées for freezing, as well as for mincing meat and chopping up cooked or raw vegetables extra finely (a useful trick if your child becomes fussy as she gets older). Many food processors have a mini bowl attachment, which will work better with smaller quantities.

Mouli This is a hand-turned food mill, ideal for foods with a tough skin, like peas or dried apricots, as you can produce a smooth purée and separate any indigestible husks or skins. Puréeing potato in a food processor tends to break down the starches and produces a sticky glutinous pulp, so potato should be puréed using a mouli or potato ricer, for a really creamy, lump-free mash. (If you don't have a mouli, you can push food through a metal sieve using the underside of a soup ladle.)

Ice-cube trays/mini pots It's a good idea to prepare baby purées in bulk and freeze individual portions in ice-cube trays or plastic pots, to be defrosted as required. Ice-cube trays should be covered with clingfilm, to prevent contamination.

Weaning spoons Baby's gums are sensitive and won't cope well with a hard metal spoon. You can buy small plastic weaning spoons, which are shallow and should have no sharp edges.

Weaning bowls You can buy small, heatproof weaning bowls.

Bibs Weaning can be a very messy business, so arm yourself with a selection of bibs. Those with sleeves give good protection, wipe-clean bibs save on washing and plastic pelican bibs with a trough are ideal for older babies.

Bouncy chair   A small bouncy chair that supports your baby's back is ideal for the first stage of weaning.

Methods of cooking
Steaming or microwaving vegetables and fruit are the best ways to preserve their fresh taste and vitamins. Vitamin C and the B vitamins are water soluble, and can easily be destroyed by overcooking, especially if they are boiled for a long time.

Steaming   Chop the vegetables or fruit, and steam until tender. If you don't have a steamer, you can use a colander over a saucepan of boiling water, with a well-fitting lid.

Microwaving   Put the chopped vegetables or fruit in a suitable dish. Add a little water, cover, leaving an air vent, and cook on full power until tender. Purée to the desired consistency and stir well to remove any hot spots.

Boiling   Just cover the chopped vegetables or fruit with water. Take care not to overcook them. Drain, retaining enough of the cooking liquid to make a smooth purée. Vegetables that are grown underground should be put into a saucepan of cold water, then brought to the boil; those that are grown above ground should be dropped into boiling water.

Baking If you're using the oven, you could take the opportunity to bake a potato, sweet potato or butternut squash for your baby. Baking root vegetables caramelizes the natural sugars, giving a lovely sweet flavour.

Freezing

It can be very difficult to blend small quantities to a very smooth texture. It's much easier, and less time consuming, to prepare purées in large batches and freeze individual portions in ice-cube trays or small freezer containers.

Once the purée portions have cooled down, freeze them as soon as possible. If you freeze them in ice-cube trays, once the cubes are frozen you can knock them out and transfer them to freezer bags. Label these clearly with the contents and the date.

To defrost frozen purées, remove them from the freezer several hours or the night before a meal, and reheat in a saucepan. Alternatively, reheat in a microwave, but do make sure you stir the purée thoroughly, to remove any hot spots.

Never refreeze meals that have already been frozen, and do not reheat foods more than once. However, commercially frozen foods like frozen peas can be refrozen once they are cooked.

If frozen at −18°C (−0.4°F), baby purées will keep for up to three months.

Hygiene

Feeding bottles should be washed and sterilized until your baby is twelve months old. There's no need to sterilize weaning bowls and spoons, but it's best to wash them in a dishwasher. Always dry them using a clean tea towel.

Any surfaces that come into contact with your baby's food – for example, the highchair tray – should be wiped with an anti-bacterial agent every day.

When you reheat your baby's food, make sure it's piping hot all the way through; food that hasn't been brought to a high temperature provides the perfect breeding ground for bacteria. Let the food cool down, then test the temperature before you feed your baby.

Don't save any half-eaten food, as saliva carries bacteria, which will have been introduced from the spoon.

Drinks

Babies' bodies contain a high percentage of water, and lose more water from their skin and kidneys than adults, so it's vital to keep them hydrated. The only drink that's suitable for your baby in the first six months, apart from breast or formula milk, is boiled, cooled tap water. Bottled mineral water, or repeatedly boiled water, can contain high concentrations of mineral salts, which are unsuitable for young babies. High levels of nitrates, sulphates and fluoride should be avoided. Sparkling water is also unsuitable for babies.

Feeding cups

It's best to reserve your baby's bottle for milk feeds. Comfort-sucking on sweetened drinks is the main cause of tooth decay in young children. It's a good idea to start using a lidded cup with a spout from the age of six or seven months, and eventually move on to a cup. Try to dispense with bottles by the time your baby is one year old, except from, perhaps, a bottle at bedtime.

Allergies

More and more babies are developing allergies, with most serious food allergies starting in infancy and early childhood. Milk and egg allergies are the most common, and often disappear well before adulthood. Wheat, soy, sesame, kiwi, shellfish and nuts are other common problem foods. The immune system becomes confused by these substances and, instead of ignoring harmless food proteins, it triggers a reaction that leads to the release of histamine. This causes the classic symptoms such as hives or swelling, or occasionally the more severe reaction of anaphylaxis, which is life-threatening.

Food allergies are much more common among children from families with a history of allergy. Babies who suffer from eczema are also at high risk of suffering from food allergies. The more severe the eczema, and the earlier the onset, the more likely there is to be a food allergy. Babies who develop severe eczema before the age of three months are very likely to suffer from food allergies. In this situation, you would need to be particularly cautious when introducing new foods, and leave a day or two between each one, to see if there's a reaction. Exclusive breast-feeding for six months may also help to prevent allergies in susceptible babies.

If you suspect that your child has an allergy, it's important to take her to have tests, rather than restricting foods that may not be causing the problem. It's never a good idea to restrict a child's diet without good reason.

There is no convincing scientific evidence to suggest that allergies can be reduced by avoiding or delaying the introduction of potentially allergenic foods beyond six months.

Immediate allergies

Most immediate food allergies are caused by milk, egg, peanuts, tree nuts, fish, shellfish or wheat. As soon as the food is eaten (often for the first or second time), an itchy rash develops, usually around the mouth. There may also be swelling of the face, a runny nose, itchiness and vomiting. A severe reaction may also cause breathing difficulties, in which case an ambulance should be called immediately. Fortunately, severe reactions are very rare in young children.

Delayed allergies

Some food allergies are more subtle and can be difficult to detect, especially if the symptoms don't develop straight away. Delayed allergies in infants may cause chronic symptoms such as eczema, reflux, colic, poor growth, diarrhoea or constipation, and symptoms will continue until the problem food is removed from the diet. The most common culprits are milk, soy, egg and wheat. However, all of these symptoms are common during childhood, and an allergy is only one explanation. Trying to work out if the problem is due to a food allergy can be very difficult and requires the help of an experienced doctor.

Cow's milk allergy
CMA is the most common food allergy among infants and young children, and presents with a variety of symptoms such as a rash or reflux. However, as these can also indicate other problems, an allergy to cow's milk can be missed as a cause.

There are two types of CMA: immediate and delayed. Both are triggered by an adverse response from the immune system. Immediate CMA typically begins within minutes of exposure to cow's milk protein, and symptoms include reflux (which causes crying, back-arching and regurgitation after feeds), diarrhoea and, in severe cases, sudden wheezing, coughing or shortness of breath. If your child has any of these symptoms, alert your GP immediately. For more information about delayed CMA, see 'Delayed allergies', left.

High-risk foods
Eggs
Thoroughly cooked eggs can be given from six months – both the white and the yolk must be solid. Soft-boiled eggs can be given from one year.

Fruits

Some children have an adverse reaction to citrus, berries and kiwi fruit, but these foods rarely cause a true allergy. The most common symptoms are vomiting, diarrhoea, asthma, eczema, hay fever, rashes and swelling of the eyes, lips and face.

Nuts

Peanuts and peanut products can induce a severe allergic reaction, which can be life-threatening. It's therefore very important to be cautious if there is a family history of allergy, including hay fever, eczema and asthma. If you have any concerns, have your baby tested for any allergies before introducing nuts.

For babies with no allergy concerns, peanut butter and finely ground nuts can be introduced from six months. Scientists have noticed that the incidence of peanut allergy in the UK, where small children tend to avoid peanuts, is relatively high, whereas in countries like Israel, where children regularly eat a peanut-based snack called Bamba, it's almost unheard of.

Whole, or chopped, nuts shouldn't be given to children under the age of five years, due to the risk of choking.

Gluten

Gluten is found in various grains, including wheat, rye and oats. Foods containing gluten, such as bread and pasta, can be introduced between six and seven months. However, if you're concerned about gluten allergy, avoid giving baby cereals containing gluten; baby rice is the safest to try first. In some cases, intolerance to wheat can be temporary, and children sometimes grow out of it. However, some people suffer from a permanent sensitivity to gluten, known as coeliac disease, which can be diagnosed with a blood test.

The good news is that children normally outgrow allergies to milk and egg (around 50 per cent by four to six years). However, some allergies last longer, and allergies to nut, fish and shellfish are less commonly outgrown. Never be afraid to take your baby to the doctor if you are worried that something is wrong.

Remember: what you feed your child today will determine his future tomorrow.

First Tastes

First vegetables

First vegetable purée

Put the carrots in a steamer set over boiling water. Cover and steam for 15–20 minutes until the carrots are really tender.

Transfer the carrots to a food processor or blender and add a little water from the steamer or some of your baby's usual milk. Purée to a smooth consistency that is quite runny and easy for your baby to swallow.

Spoon some of the purée into your baby's bowl and serve lukewarm.

/ 5 MINUTES

🖿 15–20 MINUTES

🕒 4 PORTIONS

❋ SUITABLE FOR FREEZING

2 medium carrots, peeled and sliced
a little breast milk or formula milk (optional)

Carrots make the perfect first food for your baby. They contain plenty of nutrients, and have a sweet taste and smooth texture. You can use this method for other root vegetables, such as sweet potato, parsnip or swede, although cooking times may vary.

Trio of root vegetables

🖊 7 MINUTES

⬚ 20 MINUTES

🍴 5 PORTIONS

❄ SUITABLE FOR FREEZING

2 medium carrots (175 g/
6 oz), peeled and chopped
175 g (6 oz) sweet potato
or pumpkin, peeled and
chopped
1 medium parsnip (100 g/
3½ oz), peeled and
chopped
300 ml (½ pint) boiling
water
a little breast milk or
formula milk (optional)

Put the vegetables into a saucepan and cover
with the boiling water. Cover with a lid and cook
over a medium heat for about 20 minutes, or
until tender. Strain the vegetables, then blend
to a purée with enough cooking liquid to make
a smooth consistency. If you wish, you could
also add a little of your baby's usual milk.

Alternatively, steam the vegetables, then
blend to a purée with some of the water from
the bottom of the steamer.

*Parsnips provide a good source of starch and fibre.
They also contain the antioxidant vitamins C and E.*

Potato

🔪 5 MINUTES
⊟ 20 MINUTES
🍽 6 PORTIONS
❄ SUITABLE FOR FREEZING

400 g (14 oz) potatoes,
  peeled and chopped
a little breast milk or
  formula milk (optional)

Put the potatoes into a saucepan and add
enough boiling water to just cover them.
Bring the water back to the boil and simmer
for 15 minutes, or until tender. Alternatively,
steam the potatoes until tender.

Use a mouli or potato ricer to purée the
potato, then blend with a little of the cooking
liquid or your baby's usual milk to make the
desired consistency.

*Potatoes have a mild flavour and are a good
source of vitamin C and potassium, so they are
ideal for weaning. Avoid using a food processor
to purée potato, as it breaks down the starch to
produce a sticky pulp.*

Baked sweet potato

Preheat the oven to 200°C/400°F/Gas 6. Scrub the sweet potatoes and prick the skins with a metal skewer or fork. Place them on a baking sheet and put them in the oven for about 45 minutes, or until wrinkled and tender.

Remove the potatoes from the oven, cut them in half, scoop out the flesh and purée in a food processor until smooth. To make a thinner consistency, you could add a little of your baby's usual milk.

✐ 1 MINUTE

▦ 45 MINUTES

◷ 6 PORTIONS

✳ SUITABLE FOR FREEZING

2 medium sweet potatoes
   (about 500 g/1lb 2 oz)
a little breast milk or
   formula milk (optional)

You can also use this method to bake potatoes. They tend to take longer to cook than sweet potatoes, so put them in the oven for 1–1¼ hours.

Roast butternut squash

Preheat the oven to 200°C/400°F/Gas 6. Brush the sliced sides of the butternut squash with oil, then put the halves of squash, sliced side up, in a shallow ovenproof dish. Pour in some water – it should be about 1 cm (⅓ in) deep. Put the squash in the oven for 45 minutes to 1 hour.

Remove the dish from the oven and allow the squash to cool. Scoop out the flesh and purée to the desired consistency. You can add a little of your baby's usual milk if you wish.

 5 MINUTES

 45–60 MINUTES

6 PORTIONS

SUITABLE FOR FREEZING

1 medium butternut squash
(about 700 g/1½ lb),
halved and deseeded
a little sunflower oil
a little breast milk or
formula milk (optional)

You could roast pumpkin following this method. Use half a small pumpkin and cut it into about four wedges.

Roasting butternut squash or pumpkin brings out the natural sugars and flavour. Both make good first weaning foods, as they are easily digested and are unlikely to cause allergies. Pop some in the oven when you are cooking a meal for the family.

Sweet potato and squash

/ 10 MINUTES

▭ 1 HOUR

◉ 5 PORTIONS

❄ SUITABLE FOR FREEZING

1 small or ½ large butternut
squash (about 500 g/
1 lb 2 oz), peeled, deseeded
and cut into 2.5 cm (1 in)
cubes

1 medium sweet potato
(about 450 g/1 lb), peeled
and cut into 2.5 cm (1 in)
cubes

a generous knob of butter
or margarine

2 tablespoons water

a little breast or formula
milk (optional)

Preheat the oven to 200°C/400°F/Gas 6. Lay a
large sheet of aluminium foil on a baking sheet
and spread out the squash and sweet potato on
top. Dot the butter or margarine over the
vegetables and sprinkle with the water. Lift the
sides of the foil and scrunch them together to
make a loose parcel. Bake for about 1 hour, or
until the vegetables are tender.

Allow the squash and sweet potato to cool
slightly, then transfer to a blender, along with
any cooking liquid. Blend to a smooth purée. If
you wish, you can add a little breast or formula
milk to make a thinner consistency.

*The orange flesh of sweet potato and butternut
squash is rich in betacarotene, the plant form of
vitamin A. This helps to boost the immune system,
giving protection from colds and flu.*

Parsnip, carrot and pear

Put the vegetables into a small saucepan and cover with water. Bring to the boil, cover and simmer for 15 minutes, until tender. Alternatively, steam the vegetables for about 20 minutes. Drain, reserving the water. Add the pear and blend until smooth, adding about 2 tablespoons of the cooking water, or enough to make a smooth purée.

✏ 5 MINUTES

▥ 20 MINUTES

🍳 4 PORTIONS

❄ SUITABLE FOR FREEZING

1 medium carrot (100 g/
   3½ oz), peeled and chopped
1 medium parsnip (75 g/
   3 oz), peeled and chopped
1 small pear (75 g/3 oz),
   peeled, cored and diced

Parsnip and apple

Put the parsnip and apple into a saucepan and just cover with cold water. Bring to the boil, cover and simmer for about 10 minutes, until very soft. Drain, reserving some of the cooking water, then blend using an electric hand blender. Add 1–2 teaspoons of the reserved liquid to make a smooth consistency.

✏ 10 MINUTES

▥ 15 MINUTES

🍳 3 PORTIONS

❄ SUITABLE FOR FREEZING

450 g (1 lb) parsnips, peeled
   and chopped
100 g (3½ oz) dessert
   apple, peeled, cored and
   chopped

Left: Parsnip, carrot and pear

Fruity butternut squash

Butternut squash and apple

/ 10 MINUTES

▦ 12 MINUTES

◉ 6 PORTIONS

❋ SUITABLE FOR FREEZING

350 g (12 oz) butternut
squash, peeled, deseeded
and chopped

1 medium-size sweet
dessert apple (about 125 g/
4½ oz), peeled, cored and
chopped

Put the butternut squash into a steamer and
cook for 6 minutes, then add the apple and cook
for another 6 minutes. Transfer to a blender with
about 2 tablespoons of the water from the
steamer, and purée until smooth.

Butternut squash and pear

/ 10 MINUTES

▦ 12 MINUTES

◉ 6 PORTIONS

❋ SUITABLE FOR FREEZING

350 g (12 oz) butternut
squash, peeled, deseeded
and chopped

1 medium-size ripe pear,
peeled, cored and
chopped

Put the butternut squash into a steamer and
cook for 8 minutes, then add the pear and cook
for another 4 minutes. Transfer to a blender and
purée until smooth. It probably won't be
necessary to add any liquid, but, if you think the
purée is too thick, you could add a little of the
liquid from the bottom of the steamer.

Sweet potato, carrot and apricot

✏ 3 MINUTES
🗔 20 MINUTES
🍴 3 PORTIONS
❄ SUITABLE FOR FREEZING

Put the sweet potato, carrot and apricots in a saucepan. Pour over the boiling water and cover and cook for 20 minutes. Drain, and purée using an electric hand blender.

1 small sweet potato (about 250 g/9 oz), peeled and chopped
1 medium carrot (about 75 g/3 oz), peeled and sliced
30 g (1 oz) dried apricots, chopped
350 ml (12 fl oz) boiling water

Carrot, pea and potato

✏ 10 MINUTES
🗔 20 MINUTES
🍴 4 PORTIONS
❄ SUITABLE FOR FREEZING

Put the potatoes and carrot into a saucepan and just cover with cold water. Bring to the boil, cover and simmer for 10 minutes. Add the peas and continue to cook for 5 minutes, until all the vegetables are soft. Blend until smooth, using an electric hand blender.

100 g (3½ oz) potatoes, peeled and chopped
1 large carrot (150 g/5 oz), peeled and sliced
75 g (3 oz) frozen peas

Left: Sweet potato, carrot and apricot

Butternut squash, parsnip and prune

✎ 3 MINUTES
🍳 15–20 MINUTES
🥣 4 PORTIONS
❄ SUITABLE FOR FREEZING

300 g (11 oz) butternut
  squash, peeled, deseeded
  and chopped
1 small parsnip (60 g/2 oz),
  peeled and chopped
20 g (¾ oz) ready-to-eat
  dried prunes
300 ml (½ pint) boiling
  water

Put the butternut squash, parsnip and prunes
into a saucepan. Pour over the boiling water,
cover and simmer for about 12 minutes, or until
the vegetables are tender. Purée using an electric
hand blender.

Pumpkin and pear

✎ 10 MINUTES
🍳 10 MINUTES
🥣 4 PORTIONS
❄ SUITABLE FOR FREEZING

200 g (7 oz) pumpkin,
  peeled, deseeded and
  chopped
1 medium pear (100 g/
  3½ oz), peeled, cored
  and chopped
1 tablespoon baby rice

Put the pumpkin and pear into a steamer and
cook for 10 minutes, until very soft. Blend until
smooth using an electric hand blender, then stir
in the baby rice.

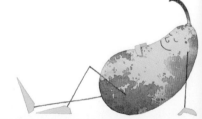

First fruit

Apple

Put the apples into a heavy-based saucepan, along with the water or apple juice. Cover, bring to the boil and simmer gently for 6–8 minutes, until really tender. Alternatively, steam the apples for 7–8 minutes.

Purée in a food processor or using a hand blender. If steaming, you could use some of the water from the bottom of the steamer to thin out the purée.

✐ 5 MINUTES

⬚ 10 MINUTES

🍴 4 PORTIONS

❄ SUITABLE FOR FREEZING

2 sweet dessert apples (such as Pink Lady, Royal Gala or Jazz), peeled, cored and chopped
4–5 tablespoons water or pure unsweetened apple juice

As a variation, you could add cinnamon. Simply add a cinnamon stick to the saucepan with the apples, then remove it before puréeing.

Pear

🔪 5 MINUTES
🗒 3–5 MINUTES
🍽 3 PORTIONS
❄ SUITABLE FOR FREEZING

2 large or 4 small ripe pears,
    peeled, cored and chopped
a little baby rice (optional)

Put the pears into a steamer and cook for
3–5 minutes. The riper they are, the quicker
they will cook. Purée using a hand blender. If the
consistency is too runny, stir in a little baby rice.

Peach, pear and baby rice

🔪 5 MINUTES
🍽 3 PORTIONS
❄ SUITABLE FOR FREEZING

1 ripe peach, skinned,
    stoned and chopped
1 ripe pear, peeled, cored
    and chopped
a little baby rice

Purée the peach and pear using a hand blender
and stir in a little baby rice.

Right: Pear

Apple and pear

Put the apples and pears into a heavy-based saucepan with the apple juice and water, cover and bring to the boil. Reduce the heat and simmer over a low heat for 6–8 minutes, until tender. Blend the fruit to a smooth purée.

 10 MINUTES

🍳 10 MINUTES

🕐 4 PORTIONS

❄ SUITABLE FOR FREEZING

2 sweet dessert apples (such as Pink Lady, Royal Gala or Jazz), peeled, cored and chopped
2 ripe pears, peeled, cored and chopped
4 tablespoons pure unsweetened apple juice
2 tablespoons water

Cream of pear

Put the pear into a small saucepan, cover and cook for 2–3 minutes. Blend until smooth. Mix together the baby rice and milk, and stir into the pear purée.

✎ 5 MINUTES

🍳 5 MINUTES

🕐 2 PORTIONS

❄ SUITABLE FOR FREEZING

2 ripe pears, peeled, cored and chopped
1 tablespoon baby rice
1 tablespoon breast or formula milk

Left: Apple and pear

Avocado

🔪 3 MINUTES

🎨 1 PORTION

❄ NOT SUITABLE FOR FREEZING

1 small ripe avocado, halved
  and stoned
a little breast or formula
  milk

Scoop out the avocado flesh and mash it together with your baby's usual milk.

Papaya and banana

🔪 3 MINUTES

🎨 1 PORTION

❄ NOT SUITABLE FOR FREEZING

½ small papaya, peeled and
  deseeded
½ small ripe banana, peeled
1–2 tablespoons breast or
  formula milk (optional)

Mash the papaya together with the banana. For a thinner consistency, add a little of your baby's usual milk.

Papaya

🔪 3 MINUTES

🎨 1 PORTION

❄ SUITABLE FOR FREEZING

½ small papaya, halved and
  deseeded

Mash the flesh with a fork until smooth.

Cantaloupe melon

Scoop out the flesh of the melon, chop, and purée using a hand blender.

🖋 5 MINUTES

🍽 6 PORTIONS

❄ SUITABLE FOR FREEZING

1 ripe cantaloupe melon, halved and deseeded

Cantaloupe melon and strawberry

Scoop out the flesh of the melon and chop, then purée the melon and strawberries using an electric hand blender. Stir in the baby rice.

🖋 7 MINUTES

🍽 2 PORTIONS

❄ SUITABLE FOR FREEZING

¼ cantaloupe melon, deseeded
2 strawberries, hulled and washed
2 tablespoons baby rice

Other varieties of sweet melon are good, too. Try honeydew or Galia.
   When your baby is a little older, very ripe melon may be eaten in pieces.

Banana

3 MINUTES

1 PORTION

NOT SUITABLE FOR FREEZING

½ small ripe banana, peeled
a little breast or formula
    milk (optional)

Simply mash the banana with a fork until
smooth. If this is too thick for your baby, you
could add a little of your baby's usual milk.

Banana and avocado

4 MINUTES

1 PORTION

NOT SUITABLE FOR FREEZING

½ small ripe avocado,
    stoned
½ small ripe banana, peeled
    and sliced
a little breast or formula
    milk (optional)

Scoop out the avocado flesh and mash together
with the banana. For a thinner consistency, stir
in a little of your baby's usual milk.

Right: Banana and avocado

Mango

Remove the skin from the mango and cut all the flesh off the stone – you should have about 115 g (4 oz) of flesh. Purée using an electric hand blender.

 5 MINUTES
 2 PORTIONS
 SUITABLE FOR FREEZING

½ medium-size ripe mango

Mango and banana

Prepare the mango as above. Purée together with the banana using an electric hand blender.

 5 MINUTES
 2 PORTIONS
 NOT SUITABLE FOR FREEZING

½ small ripe mango
½ small banana, peeled
  and sliced

Known as 'the king of fruit', mango is an antioxidant – a rich health booster.

Left: Mango

Meal planner

	Day 1	Day 2	Day 3
Breakfast	Breast/bottle	Breast/bottle	Breast/bottle
Mid-morning	Breast/bottle	Breast/bottle	Breast/bottle
Lunch	**First vegetable purée (carrot)** Breast/bottle	**First vegetable purée (sweet potato)** Breast/bottle	**Apple** Breast/bottle
Tea	Breast/bottle	Breast/bottle	Breast/bottle
Bedtime	Breast/bottle	Breast/bottle	Breast/bottle

This meal planner is intended to be used as a guide, and will depend on many factors, including weight and age. Some babies may be happy with one solid feed a day, whereas others may eat a second meal at teatime.

Day 4	Day 5	Day 6	Day 7
Breast/bottle	Breast/bottle	Breast/bottle	Breast/bottle
Breast/bottle	Breast/bottle	Breast/bottle	Breast/bottle
First vegetable purée (sweet potato) Breast/bottle	Pear Breast/bottle	Roast butternut squash Breast/bottle	Apple and pear Breast/bottle
Breast/bottle	Breast/bottle	Breast/bottle	Breast/bottle
Breast/bottle	Breast/bottle	Breast/bottle	Breast/bottle

After First Tastes

After first vegetables

Courgette

Courgette skins are soft, so don't need to be removed. Steam the courgettes for about 10 minutes, until tender, then purée using a hand blender or mash with a fork. Courgette is good mixed with sweet potato, carrot or baby rice.

✐ 5 MINUTES
🍲 10 MINUTES
🕓 8 PORTIONS
❄ SUITABLE FOR FREEZING

2 medium courgettes, washed, topped and tailed, and sliced

Broccoli and cauliflower

Put the broccoli and cauliflower into a steamer and cook for about 10 minutes, until tender. Purée until smooth, adding a little water from the steamer or some of your baby's usual milk to make the desired consistency.

Broccoli and cauliflower are good mixed with a root vegetable purée like carrot or sweet potato.

✐ 7 MINUTES
🍲 10 MINUTES
🕓 4 PORTIONS
❄ SUITABLE FOR FREEZING

50 g (2 oz) broccoli, washed and cut into small florets
50 g (2 oz) cauliflower, washed and cut into small florets
a little breast or formula milk

Courgette and broccoli (with or without cauliflower) are good mixed with sweet root vegetables like sweet potato or carrot.

✏️ 12 MINUTES

🍳 15 MINUTES

🕒 3 PORTIONS

🍊 SUITABLE FOR FREEZING

1 small sweet potato (225 g/
8 oz), peeled and chopped
1 medium carrot (about
75 g/3 oz), peeled and
chopped
2 tablespoons tinned or
frozen sweetcorn, cooked

Sweet potato, carrot and sweetcorn

Put the sweet potato and carrot into a steamer
and cook for about 15 minutes, or until tender.
Purée together with the sweetcorn and
4 tablespoons of water from the bottom
of the steamer.

✏️ 12 MINUTES

🍳 15 MINUTES

🕒 6 PORTIONS

🍊 SUITABLE FOR FREEZING

1 medium carrot (100 g/
3½ oz), peeled and sliced
200 g (7 oz) butternut
squash, peeled, deseeded
and chopped
½ small dessert apple (50 g/
2 oz), peeled, cored and
chopped
10 g (¼ oz) prunes, chopped

Butternut squash, carrot and apple

Put the carrot and squash into a steamer and
cook for 5 minutes. Add the apple and prunes
and continue to steam for 10 minutes, until all
the ingredients are tender. Blend with about
2 tablespoons of water from the steamer.

Right: Butternut squash, carrot and apple

Sweet potato with broccoli and peas

Steam the sweet potato for 3 minutes. Add the broccoli florets and steam for another 4 minutes. Add the frozen peas and steam for 3 minutes. Blitz the vegetables using an electric hand blender, together with about 75 ml (2½ fl oz) of the water from the bottom of the steamer.

/ 7 MINUTES

⬚ 10 MINUTES

🍳 3 PORTIONS

❄ SUITABLE FOR FREEZING

1 small sweet potato (300 g/ 11 oz), peeled and chopped
60 g (2 oz) broccoli florets, washed
40 g (1½ oz) frozen peas

Butternut squash, sweetcorn and peas

Steam the butternut squash for 12 minutes, until soft. Add the sweetcorn and peas and cook for another 4 minutes. Blend the vegetables using a hand blender, and stir in 2 tablespoons of water from the steamer.

/ 7 MINUTES

⬚ 16 MINUTES

🍳 5 PORTIONS

❄ SUITABLE FOR FREEZING

350 g (12 oz) butternut squash, peeled, deseeded and chopped
30 g (1 oz) tinned or frozen sweetcorn
50 g (2 oz) frozen peas

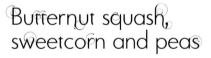

Left: Sweet potato with broccoli and peas

leek, swede, sweet potato and sweetcorn

🔪 10 MINUTES

🗓 20 MINUTES

🍪 4–6 PORTIONS

❄ SUITABLE FOR FREEZING

a knob of butter
1 medium leek, washed, peeled and chopped
125 g (4½ oz) swede, peeled and chopped
100 g (3½ oz) sweet potato, peeled and chopped
50 g (2 oz) tinned or frozen sweetcorn
250 ml (8 fl oz) breast or formula milk
200 ml (7 fl oz) water

Melt the butter in a saucepan. Add the leek and fry for 2 minutes, then add the remaining ingredients. Cover, bring to the boil, then simmer for 15 minutes, until all the vegetables are tender. Blend until smooth, using an electric hand blender.

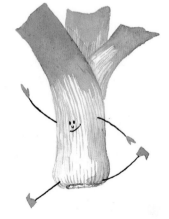

Butternut squash, pear and apricot

🔪 5 MINUTES
🍳 20 MINUTES
🍽 3 PORTIONS
❄ SUITABLE FOR FREEZING

Put all the ingredients into a saucepan, cover and bring to the boil. Reduce the heat and cook for 15 minutes, until softened.

300 g (11 oz) butternut squash, peeled, deseeded and chopped
1 medium-size ripe pear, peeled, cored and chopped
15 g (½ oz) dried apricots, chopped
200 ml (7 fl oz) boiling water

Sweet potato and apple

🔪 5 MINUTES
🍳 10 MINUTES
🍽 3 PORTIONS
❄ SUITABLE FOR FREEZING

Prick the sweet potato with a fork and microwave on High for 8–10 minutes, until soft.

Meanwhile, put the apple and the water into a heavy-based saucepan. Cover, bring to the boil, then simmer for 7–9 minutes, until softened.

Cut the sweet potato in half and scoop out the flesh. Blend with the apple and 5–6 tablespoons of water to make a smooth consistency.

1 medium sweet potato (about 450 g/1 lb), scrubbed
2 medium-size sweet dessert apples, peeled, cored and chopped
5–6 tablespoons water

Left: Butternut squash, pear and apricot

After first fruit

Apple, strawberry and banana

Put all the ingredients in a saucepan and cook over a low heat for about 8 minutes, or until the apples are tender. Purée using an electric hand blender.

✎ 5 MINUTES

▭ 10 MINUTES

🍪 3 PORTIONS

❄ SUITABLE FOR FREEZING

2 small sweet dessert apples (about 175 g/6 oz peeled weight), peeled, cored and chopped
60 g (2 oz) strawberries, hulled and quartered
½ small banana, peeled and chopped

Blueberry and banana

Melt the butter in a saucepan. Add the remaining ingredients and stir until the blueberries have softened (about 3 minutes). Blend until smooth, using an electric hand blender.

✎ 5 MINUTES

▭ 5 MINUTES

🍪 2 PORTIONS

❄ NOT SUITABLE FOR FREEZING

a small knob of butter
100 g (3½ oz) blueberries, washed
2 small bananas, peeled and chopped
2 tablespoons cold water

Apricot, apple, pear and vanilla

🔪 8 MINUTES

🍳 7–8 MINUTES

🍪 3 PORTIONS

❄ SUITABLE FOR FREEZING

75 g (3 oz) dried apricots, chopped

1 large dessert apple (150 g/ 5 oz), peeled, cored and chopped

3 tablespoons apple juice

2 tablespoons water

a few drops of vanilla extract

1 large ripe pear (about 200 g/7 oz), peeled, cored and chopped

Put the apricots and apple into a heavy-based saucepan, together with the apple juice, water and vanilla extract. Bring to the boil, then cover and simmer for 4 minutes. Add the pear and simmer for another 2–3 minutes. Purée using a electric hand blender.

Dried apricots are one of nature's superfoods. The drying process concentrates the goodness of the fruit. They are an excellent source of iron and are also rich in vitamins A and C.

When preparing dried fruit like apricots and raisins for young babies, it should be put through a mouli to get rid of the outer skin, as it's difficult to digest.

Apple, pear, blueberry and vanilla

Put all the ingredients into a heavy-based saucepan. Cover and cook over a low heat for about 6 minutes. Purée in a blender.

✎ 7 MINUTES

▢ 6 MINUTES

◔ 2 PORTIONS

✳ SUITABLE FOR FREEZING

1 sweet dessert apple, peeled, cored and chopped
1 ripe pear, peeled, cored and chopped
40 g (1½ oz) blueberries, washed
¼ teaspoon vanilla extract

Apple, apricot and pear

Put the apple and dried apricots in a saucepan with the water. Cover, bring to the boil and simmer for 5 minutes. Add the pear and simmer for another 2 minutes. Purée until smooth.

In a small bowl, mix the baby rice with the milk until smooth, then stir into the fruit purée.

Apple, apricot and pear is good with mashed banana. It should be mixed into the purée just before serving. Banana isn't suitable for freezing.

✎ 8 MINUTES

▢ 10 MINUTES

◔ 2 PORTIONS

✳ SUITABLE FOR FREEZING

1 dessert apple, peeled, cored and chopped
60 g (2 oz) dried apricots, roughly chopped
4 tablespoons water
1 ripe pear, peeled, cored and chopped
1 tablespoon baby rice
2 tablespoons breast or formula milk

Left: Apple, pear, blueberry and vanilla

Peach, apple, pear and banana

📝 7 MINUTES

🍳 7 MINUTES

🍽 3 PORTIONS

❄ SUITABLE FOR FREEZING

1 ripe peach, skinned (*see box below*), stoned and chopped
1 dessert apple, peeled, cored and chopped
1 pear, peeled, cored and chopped
1 small banana, peeled and sliced
4 tablespoons water

Put all the ingredients into a heavy-based saucepan. Cover and cook over a low heat for about 7 minutes, or until the apple is soft. Blend to a purée using an electric hand blender.

To remove the skin from any soft fruit such as a peach, cut a cross in the base using a sharp knife. Put in a bowl and cover with boiling water. Leave for 1 minute. Drain and rinse in cold water. The skin should peel off easily.

Apple and raisin compote

Heat the orange juice in a saucepan, then add the apples and raisins. Cook on a low heat for about 5 minutes, until soft, adding a little water if necessary. Purée using a blender.

🔪 5 MINUTES
🍳 6 MINUTES
🎨 8 PORTIONS
❄ SUITABLE FOR FREEZING

3 tablespoons freshly squeezed orange juice
2 dessert apples, peeled, cored and sliced
15 g (½ oz) raisins, washed

Nectarine, banana and porridge

In a small bowl, mix the porridge with the cooled boiled water. Blitz the nectarine and banana with an electric hand blender and stir into the porridge.

🔪 5 MINUTES
🍳 20 MINUTES
🎨 1 PORTION
❄ NOT SUITABLE FOR FREEZING

1 tablespoon baby porridge
1 tablespoon cooled boiled water
1 ripe nectarine, skinned, stoned and chopped
½ small ripe banana, peeled and sliced

Left: Nectarine, banana and porridge

Porridge with apple, pear and raisins

⟋ 7 MINUTES

▦ 10 MINUTES

🕒 3 PORTIONS

❄ SUITABLE FOR FREEZING

2 dessert apples, peeled, cored and chopped
2 ripe pears, peeled, cored and chopped
30 g (1 oz) raisins
4 tablespoons water
2 tablespoons baby porridge
2 tablespoons cooled boiled water

Put the apple, pear and raisins into a heavy-based saucepan, together with the water. Cover, bring to the boil, reduce the heat and simmer for about 8 minutes, or until the apples are soft. Purée using an electric hand blender.

Mix the baby porridge with the cooled boiled water and stir into the purée.

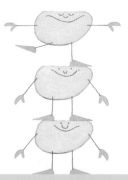

Pears are one of the least allergenic foods, making them great for weaning.

Plum

/ 5 MINUTES

⬚ 5 MINUTES

◔ 1 PORTION

✳ SUITABLE FOR FREEZING

2 large ripe plums, skinned,
  stoned and chopped
a little baby rice, crumbled
  rusk or mashed banana

Purée the plums uncooked if ripe and juicy,
or steam for a few minutes until tender. Mix
with some baby rice, crumbled rusk or mashed
banana.

Plum and apple

/ 8 MINUTES

⬚ 12 MINUTES

◔ 2 PORTIONS

✳ SUITABLE FOR FREEZING

3 ripe plums (150 g/5 oz),
  skinned, stoned and
  chopped
2 dessert apples, peeled,
  cored and chopped
6 tablespoons water
30 g (1 oz) sultanas

Put all the ingredients into a small saucepan.
Bring to the boil, reduce the heat and simmer
for 10 minutes, or until soft. Blend until smooth.

Plum, peach and banana

Put the fruit into a heavy-based saucepan and cook over a low heat for about 4 minutes, until softened. Purée using a blender.

✎ 10 MINUTES

▣ 4 MINUTES

🍴 3 PORTIONS

❄ SUITABLE FOR FREEZING

4 ripe, sweet plums (200 g/ 7 oz), skinned, stoned and chopped
1 large ripe peach (150 g/ 5 oz), skinned, stoned and chopped
1 small banana, peeled and sliced

Peach and banana

Mash the peach together with the banana, using a fork or a hand blender. Serve on its own or mixed with a little baby rice.

✎ 10 MINUTES

🍴 3 PORTIONS

❄ NOT SUITABLE FOR FREEZING

You could use nectarines instead of peaches. Sweet white nectarines are especially good.

1 ripe juicy peach, skinned and stoned
½ small ripe banana
a little baby rice (optional)

Peach

- 🔪 10 MINUTES
- 🍽 3 PORTIONS
- ❄ SUITABLE FOR FREEZING

1 ripe juicy peach, skinned and stoned
a little baby rice (optional)

Mash the peach, or purée using an electric hand blender. You may want to stir in a little baby rice, as it will probably be very runny.

Mango and strawberry

- 🔪 5 MINUTES
- 🍽 3 PORTIONS
- ❄ SUITABLE FOR FREEZING

½ small ripe mango
2 strawberries, washed and hulled

Remove the skin from the mango and cut the flesh off the stone. Blend the mango together with the strawberries.

Peach and blueberry

- 🔪 10 MINUTES
- ▭ 5 MINUTES
- 🍽 2 PORTIONS
- ❄ SUITABLE FOR FREEZING

2 medium-size ripe peaches, skinned, stoned and chopped
40 g (1½ oz) blueberries

Put the peaches and blueberries into a saucepan and cook over a medium heat for 3 minutes. Blend to a purée.

Baby biscotti

Preheat the oven to 180°C/350°F/Gas 4. Line a baking sheet with non-stick baking paper.

Cream the butter and sugar together using an electric hand mixer or a wooden spoon, then add the egg, flour, baking powder and cinnamon. Combine well to form a dough, then knead on a floured work surface for 5 minutes, until the dough is smooth and no longer sticky.

Divide the dough into 2 pieces and roll out each half to 18 x 4 cm (7 x 1½ in) and 2 cm (¾ in) deep. Place them on the prepared baking sheet and put them in the oven for 25 minutes.

The dough will now look like large sausages. Remove them from the oven and cut into slices 2 cm (¾ in) thick. Spread them out on the baking sheet and return to the oven for 20 minutes, turning over halfway through the cooking time.

✏ 10 MINUTES
🗓 45 MINUTES
🍪 20 BISCOTTI
✱ SUITABLE FOR FREEZING

50 g (2 oz) butter, softened
50 g (2 oz) light brown sugar
1 egg
150 g (5 oz) plain flour
1 teaspoon baking powder
½ teaspoon cinnamon

You can serve these with any fruit purée.

Meal planner

	Day 1	Day 2	Day 3
Early morning	Breast/bottle	Breast/bottle	Breast/bottle
Breakfast	Peach, apple, pear and banana	Nectarine, banana and porridge	Apple, strawberry and banana
Mid-morning	Breast/bottle	Breast/bottle	Breast/bottle
Lunch	Sweet potato with broccoli and peas	Leek, swede, sweet potato and sweetcorn	Butternut squash, sweetcorn and peas
Mid-afternoon	Breast/bottle	Breast/bottle	Breast/bottle
Dinner	Butternut squash, carrot and apple	Sweet potato and apple	Baby biscotti Apple, apricot and pear
Bedtime	Breast/bottle	Breast/bottle	Breast/bottle

This meal planner is intended to be used as a guide, and will depend on many factors, including weight and age. Some babies will manage to eat some fruit after lunch or dinner.

Day 4	Day 5	Day 6	Day 7
Breast/bottle	Breast/bottle	Breast/bottle	Breast/bottle
Porridge with apple, pear and raisins	Apple, pear, blueberry and vanilla	Peach and banana	Blueberry and banana
Breast/bottle	Breast/bottle	Breast/bottle	Breast/bottle
Butternut squash, pear and apricot	Leek, swede, sweet potato and sweetcorn	Butternut squash, sweetcorn and peas	Butternut squash, carrot and apple
Breast/bottle	Breast/bottle	Breast/bottle	Breast/bottle
Sweet potato with broccoli and peas	Butternut squash, carrot and apple	Sweet potato and apple	Sweet potato with broccoli and peas
Breast/bottle	Breast/bottle	Breast/bottle	Breast/bottle

Index

About Annabel Karmel

Mother of three, Annabel Karmel MBE is the UK's number one parenting author and expert on devising delicious, nutritious meals for babies, toddlers and children.

Since launching with *The Complete Baby and Toddler Meal Planner* more than two decades ago, Annabel has written 37 books, which have sold over 4 million copies worldwide, covering every stage of a child's development.

With the sole aim of helping parents give their children the very best start in life, Annabel's tried-and-tested recipes have also grown into a successful supermarket food range. From delicious Organic Baby Purées to her best-selling healthy chilled meals, these offer the goodness of a home-cooked meal for those busy days.

Annabel was awarded an MBE in 2006, in the Queen's Birthday Honours, for her outstanding work in child nutrition. She also has menus in some of the largest leisure resorts in Britain and a successful app, *Annabel's Essential Guide to Feeding Your Baby and Toddler.*

For more information and recipes, visit **www.annabelkarmel.com**.

Acknowledgements

Louise Ward and Phil Carroll (Sainsbury's Books), Fiona MacIntyre, Martin Higgins and Cat Dowlett (Ebury), Dave King (photography), Tamsin Weston (props), Kate Bliman and Maud Eden (food stylists), Lucinda McCord (recipe testing), Nick Eddison and Katie Golsby (Eddison Sadd), and Sarah Smith (PR).

annabel karmel

Other titles in the series are:

ANNABEL KARMEL'S FAVOURITES

Exploring new tastes

Introduce your baby to new flavours and textures

Suitable from six to nine months

ANNABEL KARMEL'S FAVOURITES

Growing independence

Healthy home-made recipes to encourage self-feeding

Suitable from nine to twelve months

ANNABEL KARMEL'S FAVOURITES

Toddler meals

Nutritious recipes for your child to enjoy with the family

Suitable from one year

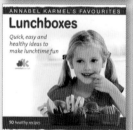

ANNABEL KARMEL'S FAVOURITES

Lunchboxes

Quick, easy and healthy ideas to make lunchtime fun

50 healthy recipes

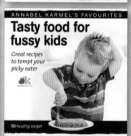

ANNABEL KARMEL'S FAVOURITES

Tasty food for fussy kids

Great recipes to tempt your picky eater

50 healthy recipes

ANNABEL KARMEL'S FAVOURITES

Family meals

Quick and easy recipes to keep meal times fresh

50 healthy recipes

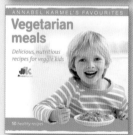

ANNABEL KARMEL'S FAVOURITES

Vegetarian meals

Delicious, nutritious recipes for veggie kids

50 healthy recipes

ANNABEL KARMEL'S FAVOURITES

Party food

Quick, quirky and fun ideas for your child's celebration

50 healthy recipes

ANNABEL KARMEL'S FAVOURITES

Kids in the Kitchen

Creative recipe ideas to make and bake together

50 healthy recipes